Early Progress Of Christianity In Buchan: Being Two Papers Read Before The Club Of Deir

George Ogilvie

Early Progress of Christianity in Buchan,

BEING TWO PAPERS READ BEFORE

THE CLUB OF DEIR,

BY

GEORGE OGILVIE, M.D.,

PROFESSOR OF THE INSTITUTES OF MEDICINE IN THE
UNIVERSITY OF ABERDEEN.

ABERDEEN:
PRINTED FOR THE CLUB,
BY ARTHUR KING & CO.
1873.

Published in

ABERDEEN, by	...	..	...	A. BROWN & CO.
EDINBURGH,	...	...	...	R. GRANT & SON.
LONDON,	...	...	...	LONGMANS & CO.

PREFACE.

THE Club of Deir is a small society of gentlemen resident in the Northern part of Buchan, which, for certain civil and ecclesiastical purposes, is designated the District of Deer—the solitary reminiscence, in our day, of the extensive supremacy once attached to the celebrated abbey of that name. The Club was founded in 1868, for the discussion of scientific, literary, and other subjects of general interest, with the view also of following out, where expedient, the conclusions arrived at, to practical effect. A list is subjoined of the members at this date.

The Communications hitherto made to the Club have had a bearing, more or less direct, on the history, social condition, and physical capabilities of the country, and comprise papers on "The Volunteer Service, as a means of culture" (Mr Mitchell), on "Cottage Hospitals" (Dr. Jamieson), on "Some points in the Chemistry of Agriculture" (Mr. Hay), on "The Condition of the Agricultural Labourer" (Dr. Gavin), on "The Tenure of Land" (Mr. Wilson), and on "The Poor Laws" (Mr Milne)—and some of these topics have been so ably handled by the authors, that in allowing his own communications to be put forth by the Club as their first publication,—though that on "Cottage Hospitals" also has appeared in another form—the remark is, in a measure, forced on the writer, that the selection is due, not to any special merit of composition, but simply to the local interest connected with some of the points involved, and to the previous direction of public attention towards them by a much abler hand, whose recent work, the Preface to the Book of Deer, has been so largely drawn upon.

Since the paper was read, he has had the opportunity of verifying some points, and adding a few others, from the notices of our local saints and worthies in the concluding part of the Collection of Scottish Calendars, just published by Dr. Forbes, Bishop of Brechin—the fullest account, taken as a whole, that has yet appeared of these lights of a dark age. Thanks are also due to Mr. Mitchell of St. Fergus, for his trouble in searching out the occasional references to the rebuilding of our parish churches, in the Minutes of the Presbytery of Deer.

BOYNDLIE, *October* 9, 1872.

THE CLUB OF DEIR.

ORDINARY MEMBERS.

Rev. J. MITCHELL, St. Fergus, *President.*

T. J. BREMNER, of Haddo.

J. COOPER, M.D., Old Deer.

W. F. CORDINER, of Cortes.

W. FERGUSON, of Kinmundy.

W. D. FORDYCE, of Brucklay, M.P.

J. D. FORDYCE, of Culsh.

W. A. GAVIN, M.R.C.S., Strichen.

W. HAY, Tillydesk.

W. HUTCHISON, of Cairngall.

P. JAMIESON, L.R.C.S., Peterhead.

Rev. A. MILNE, Tyrie.

W. D. NIVEN, M.A., Trinity College, Cambridge.

G. OGILVIE, M.D., Yr. of Boyndlie.

Rev. J. PETER, Deer.

J. WALLACE, Peterhead.

Rev. J. WILSON, Aberdour.

HONORARY MEMBERS.

W. BRUCE, M.D., DINGWALL.

A. FINDLATER, LL.D., EDINBURGH.

W. GRANT, M.B., LONDON.

J. STUART, LL.D., EDINBURGH.

Notes Bearing on the Early Progress of Christianity in Buchan.

PART I.

LTHOUGH by the rules of our Club, what may be called controversial subjects—whether in religion or politics—are judiciously excluded, yet as social questions—though bearing on politics—are not considered objectionable, but rather, on the contrary, seem generally to be the most favoured topics, as coming home so closely to our personal interests, so there are certain questions similarly related to our religious belief, which, while on this account they take a strong hold of our affections, are yet so far removed from all direct points of controversy as to be free from the risk of endangering the harmony of our meetings, and so appear to me very eligible for bringing under your consideration, both as important in themselves, and as enlarging the range of subjects coming before us, which, in so limited a circle of contributors, must else tend to become too much of the same character.

Whatever differences, unfortunately, now prevail among Christians —differences cropping out all the more prominently by reason of the freedom of expression distinguishing our age and country—still I am persuaded all earnest minded men amongst us look back with sentiments of affectionate respect to those early pioneers of the Gospel, who—though rude, it may be, as were the times in which they lived—yet with a devotion which has never been surpassed, succeeded in planting, among our forefathers, that system of faith which is the real source of our existing civilization, and of the high position we now hold among the nations of the world.

The subject, moreover, is one which has an additional relish to ourselves, in having been so much worked up by Aberdeenshire men, or those at least connected with our county ; for without disparagement of the labours of Dr. Reeves, Count Montalembert, and others, I think I may fairly say that it is mainly to the exertions, in a former generation, of Thomas Innes, the real founder of correct views on the old Celtic History of Scotland, and in our own day, of the late Dr. Joseph Robertson, Professor Innes, Dr. Stuart, Mr. J. H. Burton, Dr. Grub, and Mr Skene, that we are indebted for whatever rational and reliable information we have as to the introduction of Chris-tianity, and the general condition of the country and its inhabitants in the fifth and succeeding ages—and the few notices now to be brought forward are little more than a sort of resumè of their statements on the subject.

Archæological researches in most parts of the world where such have been made, have discovered evidence more or less conclusive, of the prior existence of races so different from the later population, as to preclude the idea of their ancestral connection, and suggest the probability of the aborigines having been supplanted by succeeding occupants either in the shock of their first collision, or by some such gradual process of extinction as we still see going on with the natives of so many of our colonial dependencies. The gigantic mounds of the American prairies, and the ruined cities of Guatemala, show this on the other side of the Atlantic as much as do the " Kitchen Middens," the instruments of flint and bronze, or even the remains of the elaborate lake dwellings in various parts of Europe.

Such relics of an antiquity which has left no trace either in history or tradition, are by no means wanting in our own country—though not so numerous or striking as in some others—and warrant the conclusion that here as elsewhere there existed a primeval population, differing in many points from that which we find in possession at the first dawn of history. The evidence may not be sufficient for concluding the relics of the stone and bronze ages to indicate the prior existence of different races, both now extinct, or for referring only the remains belonging to the later " Iron Age" to the earliest historical inhabitants, because all the three may perhaps represent only successive phases in the same community ; but certain peculiarities in the conformation of the skulls found in the oldest barrows are in favour of the opinion of the former existence here also of an aboriginal race now extinct, though it must be admitted that the evidence hitherto obtained forms but a scant foundation for the fabric some would rear upon it.

When we advance a stage further, we find the archæological gloom somewhat mitigated by the light reflected from researches into ethnography and philology. In fact, notwithstanding the flux and reflux of population in the troubled history of the world, and the migration of vast masses of people by invasion or captivity on the one hand, or in the slower but more widespread process of colonization on the other, we can still, in general, recognize the primary seats of the leading branches of mankind, and even of their principal subdivisions. Africa we recognize as the real home of the Negro, widely as that race is now spread in all the warmer regions of the earth; Central Asia is known to be the head-quarters of the Tartar or Turcoman races, for all that we have different European nations (as the Turks and Hungarians) of a kindred stock; Arabia and Syria are admitted to be the primary seats of the Semitic group of nations, notwithstanding the dispersion of the Jews through all countries, and the world wide conquests of the Arabs. So too there is a very general agreement among ethnologists that the birthplace of the European nations was also in the Asiatic continent, from which India on the one hand, and Persia and Europe on the other, were overspread by races which still retain traces of an original community of language, and present marked indications of a higher mental development. Of this great Indo-European stock the earliest westward wave of population seems to have originated the Celtic race, which in the first dawn of European history was much more widely distributed over that continent than in later times, being in turn pushed westward, and in great measure swallowed up by succeeding waves of migration, of which the German or Teutonic, and the Russian or Sclavonic races are the most conspicuous existing representatives. By the pressure especially of the former, the Celts—so far as they were not amalgamated with the invaders—were thrust eventually into Ireland, and the westmost nooks of Britain and the Continent, as Cornwall, Wales, Galloway, the Scottish Highlands, and Brittany. The languages spoken by this population of the West, though all

referable to the Celtic family, admit of a farther division into two
leading groups, indicating a corresponding diversity of origin,—the
Cymbric, which is now represented by the Welsh, and the Erse or
Gaelic of Ireland and the Highlands.

At the time when our country first comes historically into view,
in the pages of Julius Cæsar, the Celtic race, though evidently reced-
ing westward, still occupied the whole of Britain, as well as a large
tract of the Continent, including modern France, and parts of Spain
and Belgium, the Rhine being their eastern boundary; but at an
earlier period there is reason to believe that a Celtic population
inhabited the seaboard of Germany beyond that river, and reached
northwards into Scandinavia. On the whole, the balance of probability seems in favour of the natives of our Islands being all originally
Celts of the Cymbric family; but, previous to the Christian era, tribes
of Gaelic affinity seem to have effected settlements on the coasts,
and eventually to have become dominant both in North Britain and
in Ireland, and to this source we are probably to refer the two races
who make so considerable a figure in our early history—the Picts
and the Scots.

It can hardly be doubted that the Northern tribes of Britain, to
whom the name of Caledonians is applied by Tacitus, were the same
people with those known afterwards as Picts. Eumenius (A.D. 306)
who is perhaps the first writer to use this word, speaks of the " Caledonians and other Picts." Its popular derivation is from the Latin
picti (painted men)—the wild natives of the north being supposed to
have retained that old British custom after its desuetude among the
more civilized provincials of the south; and to this view the expres-

sion of Claudian in his Eulogy of Honorius, "nec falso nomine Pictos edomuit" certainly gives some colour. Neither this name, however, nor that of Caledonians was used by themselves, but Albanaich—the country being known both in Erse and Gaelic as Alba or Alban, a modification of the Albion of Pliny and of the Albany of the Scottish Peerage.

It is to the Celts of the North of Europe that Mr Skene would look as the ancestors of the Picts ; but no question perhaps in the whole range of literary discussion has given rise to more voluminous and angry discussion, than their origin and affinities,* and although the preponderating opinion of the most recent authorities is certainly in favour of their Celtic descent, some of the arguments on the Teutonic side are not easily disposed of. Such is that drawn from the conjectures of Tacitus, who, from his connection with their conqueror Agricola, had ample means of information. The features of the various tribes of Britain, he says, are so various as to warrant conclusions of a corresponding diversity of extraction—for the red hair and large limbs of the Caledonians attest a German origin ; the dark complexion and curled hair of the Silures of the South-west and their position right opposite Spain suggest their descent from some old colony of Iberians ; while those of the South-east coasts, opposite the Gauls, resemble them, making it probable that the Gauls had occupied the parts of Britain lying in their vicinity. (Life of Agricola, xi.) To this expression of opinion on the part of the

---

* Of the great Pictish Controversy with which Sir Walter Scott makes merry in "The Antiquary," a resume is given in Burton's History of Scotland (I. 5), and another, still better, though of older date, in the *Quarterly Review* of July, 1829.

Roman historian, we must add that the inhabitants of the East Coast, as far north as the Moray Firth, appear as a Teutonic people from the date of their first mention by foreign writers ; and whether the language and other peculiarities are derived from the red-haired and large-limbed Caledonians of Tacitus, or from subsequent settlements of Saxons and allied races in these parts, the fact is, as Burton remarks, that the broadest and purest Lowland Scots is spoken on the edge of the Highland line.* On the other hand, we have to bear in mind that the occupation of the country at large by a population so different in character from the Celts, has no support from the traditions or records of the latter ; and that the amount and weight of such evidence—at least from Irish sources—is not inconsiderable.

The Celtic nationality of the other race, so prominent in our early history—the Scots—is generally admitted, as well as their affinity with the Gaelic or Erse-speaking population of Scotland and Ireland of the present day. The Scots of North Britain were a colony from Ireland, to which they are conjectured by Thomas Innes to have come from the Cymbric Chersonese (Jutland), being driven out by the pressure of the advancing Teutonic tribes, but tradition assigns them rather a Spanish origin, and the probability of this, Dr. Wilson thinks, is confirmed by the historical coincidence, that the Celtic nations of Spain were reduced to great extremities by the bloody wars of the Roman subjugation in the second century, B. C., when he suggests that a body of refugees may have migrated to the shores of Celtic Ireland, and come to be known by the name of *Skuyts* or Scots, i. e.,

* Hist. Scot., Vol. I.

nomads or wanderers.*   From Ireland at a later period they spread
over to the adjacent coast of Scotland, and though in both countries
they long dwelt side by side with the older Celtic population, yet
by their superior energy they seem to have become eventually the
dominant race, and their dialect to have superseded the indigenous
language both of Scotland and Ireland.

The subjugation of South Britain by the Romans, and their occupation of it for four centuries had comparatively little effect on the
northern part of the island, which retained its independence.   Part,
however, of what is now included in Scotland was for a time reduced
to the condition of a Roman province, so that at the close of the
Imperial domination (A.D. 448), the inhabitants may be generally
arranged as follows :—

1. South of the Forth and Clyde was the Province of Valentia,
inhabited by the Romanized Britons, among whom by this time
Christianity had made considerable progress.

4. On the west coast (Argyleshire), was the Colony of the Dalriadic Scots from Ireland, who were mostly still pagans, and received
their Christianity only in the 6th century, as a sequel to the conversion of their Irish kinsmen by the labours of St. Patrick.

3. The whole of the rest of Scotland was occupied by the
original Celtic inhabitants, the Picts or Caledonians.   The Picts
South of the Month or Grampian Range—whose chief's residence was
at Forteviot in Perthshire, were partially evangelized by St. Ninian
and St. Palladius in the fourth and fifth centuries, but those of the
northern districts remained pagans for another century, and owed

* Prehistoric Annals, IV. Chap.

their conversion to Christianity, as did also the Dalriadic Scots generally, to the labours of St. Columba, who is hence deservedly reverenced as the Apostle of Scotland.

This eminent missionary, born among the Scots of Ireland, and according to Dr. Reeves in the year 521, left his native county in 563, and crossing over to Scotland in an open boat with twelve companions, founded the celebrated monastery in Iona, which was to be for many ages the beacon light of the Faith in these Isles of the West. From this as a centre he not only made frequent journeys among the Scottish Colonists, but undertook also numerous expeditions through the districts of the North and East, inhabited by the unconverted Picts, leaving, where facility was afforded him, some of his followers to establish a religious community, which might serve in after time as a fresh centre of missionary work. Thus, in co-operation with the labours in the South of his older contemporary, St. Kentigern of Glasgow, he laid the foundation of the conversion of the whole population to Christianity.

His first important expedition was to the seat of Brude, the chief or king of the Northern Picts, who had brought under his dominion also those of the South, and who from his residence at Craig Phadrick near the modern town of Inverness, extended his sway from the Forth to the extremity of Caithness, and even as it would seem to the Orkney and Western Islands. In this mission, the author of the life of St. Congall says he was accompanied by that Saint, and also by St. Cainich or Kenneth, who being both of the race of the Irish Picts of Ulster, may have been selected from their affinity to the Picts of

2

North Britain.* At his first approach, we are told by Adamnan, the king caused the gates of his residence to be shut against him, but Columba going up traced on them the sign of the cross, and struck them with his hand, whereon the bolts flew back and the Saint entered with his companions through the open doors. The king and his council, in great awe, went forward to meet him, received him with reverence, and entertained him in the most friendly way.† Columba was now allowed to preach the Gospel without hindrance, and the king became a Christian, notwithstanding the opposition of his friend and foster-father Broichan, a heathen priest, or Magician *(Magus)*, as he is termed by Adamnan. Columba made several subsequent visits to the king, and travelled also through various parts of his dominions, so that either by himself or his disciples, the Gospel before long was preached throughout the whole kingdom, and among the islands on its western and northern shores. Wherever Columba and his followers went monasteries were established on the model of Iona, and from each of these again, the Monks went forth to proclaim the glad tidings of salvation."‡ By reason of the leading part taken by the missionaries of Iona, in the evangelization both of Scots and Picts, these races, though for long after politically independent, were alike subject in matters ecclesiastical, to the Abbots of Iona.

In so far, the political and ecclesiastical relations of Scotland in general, and some of the principal details, have been well understood, since Thomas Innes cleared away the rubbish with which the

* Reeves' Adamnan, p. 153, note.   † Vita S. Columba II. 35.
‡ Grub. Ecl. His. i. 54.

subject was overlaid by the historians of the Stuart period; but till quite lately, nothing was known of the contemporaneous state of Buchan, that province lying out of the main lines of intercourse. New light has been thrown of late on this district, which, of course, has a special interest for us, by the discovery, at Cambridge, of the Book of Deer, and by the able manner in which it has just been edited by the learned Secretary of the Spalding Club. This MS. is, in the main, a copy of the Gospels, dating, probably, from the close of the 9th century—defective in part, and corrupt in the text—to which have been added, at different times, an office for the visitation of the sick, as used by the old Celtic Monks of Deer, and, what is historically of most interest, some marginal memoranda in Gaelic, of the 11th and 12th centuries, of endowments and grants to the Church of Deer, by various chiefs, clenched by a sort of confirmatory charter of David I., in Latin.

They are prefaced by the legend current with the Monks at the time of the foundation of the house, narrating the arrival at Aberdour of St. Columba, accompanied by his pupil, Drostan, but without any indication whether they reached this point in one of the skin boats, so much in use with the Saint and his followers, or were on a landward circuit, through the northern districts. It goes on to say, that the chief of the district of Buchan, who seems to have been on the spot, made an offering to the clerics of the "city" of Aberdour.*

---

* In this neighbourhood, the Editor remarks, "about a mile inland from the bay," numerous hut foundations have been discovered, some of them under a great depth of moss· In the moorland parts, both of Aberdour and Tyrie, foundations of huts are still to be seen in various places, though many have been destroyed quite lately in agricultural improve-

It is probable they tarried here some time, and founded a monastery
on the land granted them, for we find that the Church of Aberdour,
which is one of the oldest in the district, and of whose foundation we
have no record, was dedicated to St. Drostan, and up to the time of
the Reformation, boasted of possessing his relics.   Of this, however,
the legend takes no notice, but merely goes on to say that thereafter
they came to another city, which, pleasing the Saint, as full of
God's grace, he asked it in gift.   This the ruler declined, therefore,
his son became sick, and was all but dead, when the *mormàer*
besought the prayers of the clerics for his recovery, and gave them
an offering of the town, which he had formerly refused.   They com-
plied with his request, and their prayers were heard in the recovery
of the son.

On the land thus granted, the clerics founded a monastery, which
came to be known as that of Deer.

But this having been done, the Island Saint must hasten to other
districts, to diffuse the precious seed entrusted to him, and establish
other colonies of missionaries.   Before doing so, however, he transferred to Drostan all his authority over the newly-founded church.
In the words of the legend—" After that, Columcille gave to Drostan
that town, and blessed it, and left as his word, that ' whosoever

---

ments.   In a notice of the Book of Deer, in the ' Scotsman,' newspaper, of January 21,
1870, the writer, who is evidently well up in the topography of the country, mentions the
existence in one place, of whole rows of foundations, on one side of which a mound may
be traced, as if the settlement had been surrounded with a rampart.   All the foundations
are of the same shape and size, circular, and thirty-two feet across, with the door to the
south-east, the most sheltered quarter in the district.   A green spot in the middle of each,
with ashes below the turf, seems to mark the hearth.

should come against it, let him not be many-yeared [or] victorious.' Drostan's tears came, on parting with Columcille. Said Columcille, ' Let Dear be its name henceforward.' "

I believe, however, that Celtic scholars are agreed that the real derivation of Deer is from *Dair* an *Oak*, a word which we find variously modified in many names of places, as Craigendarroch (Crag of the Oaks), at Ballater. Some of St. Columba's other foundations contain in their names the same word, as Dairmag (the Field of Oaks, which Adamnan latinizes Roboretum). The country then abounded in this tree, as is shown by its remains in many of our mosses, and the names of such places as Aikie-hill and Aikie-brae, still preserve in a later dialect the remembrance of the oaks which once grew there.*

The term *Mormaer,* or High Steward, in this legend, is an evident anachronism, showing the date of the entry not to be earlier than the tenth century, when this form of territorial magistracy began in the low country to supersede that of *Toisech,* or clan-chief, who continued to hold rule in the Highlands down to the middle of last century.

St. Drostan, who was left in charge of Deer, is said, in the Aberdeen Breviary, to have been connected with the Royal Family of the Scots, and to have been sent to St. Columba before the latter left Ireland, but he is not named among the twelve who crossed over with him to Iona, and when he rejoined him in Scotland is not known. At a more advanced age, we, are told, desirous of a

---

* That the old pronunciation coincided with this derivation, is indicated by the expression, " Clerici de Dér," in the Latin of King David's charter above referred to.

stricter life, he retired to Glenesk, in Angus, where he lived as a hermit, and founded a church by the side of Lochlee.

Subsequent probably, to the time of Columba and Drostan, was the mission of St. Fergus, of which the following notice is given by the editor, in the preface to the Book of Deer—" St. Fergus, after having performed the office of a Bishop for many years in Ireland, came on a mission to the western parts of Scotland, in company with a body of Presbyters, or clerics. Arriving in the neighbour-hood of Strogeath, he and his friends settled there for a time, leading a somewhat solitary life; but seeing the country good and suitable for settlement, St. Fergus put his hands to the work, and erected three churches. From thence he pursued his course to Caithness, where he preached to the rude people of the country, and drew them to the faith, not more by the truth of its doctrine, than by the greatness of his virtues. Again, leaving Caithness, he arrived in Buchan, in the place which came commonly to be called Lungley, and where the church which he built is dedicated to his memory. Forsaking Buchan for the country of Angus, he settled at Glammis, where he erected fresh cenobia to God, choosing this as the place of his rest. Here, accordingly, he died; and here, after his death, many miracles were wrought by his relics. So great were these, that, in course of time, an Abbot of Scone, with much devotion, removed his head from his tomb, and placed it in his own monastery, at Scone, where, in like manner, miracles were wrought through the merits of St. Fergus."

This is the legendary account of the Saint, and its substantial truth is confirmed by the dedication of churches to his memory in the places stated, while the removal of the relics to Scone may be held to be established by an entry in the books of the High Treasurer of Scotland, recording an offering made by James IV. "to Sanct Fergus' heide in Scone."*

The Crozier of St. Fergus, with which he is said to have calmed a tempest, and saved his boat and crew, appears to have been preserved in the Church in Buchan, which bears his name.* Dr Forbes, Bishop of Brechin, in his collection of Scottish Calendars, just published, inclines to identify him with Fergustus, a Pictish Bishop of Scotland, who assisted at a Roman Council in 721. The principal objection is, that our Scottish hagiologists, who take most of our worthies to Rome—even such as St. Columba and St. Machar, who, there is good reason to believe, never left their own land—make no reference to such an event in the case of St. Fergus; but the Bishop suggests that it may have occurred during his episcopate in Ireland, before he appeared in North Britain.* St Fergus is commemorated in the Scottish Calendar, on November 17th.

St. Ethernan, or Eddran, to whom the Church of Rathen was dedicated, completes our list of these pioneers of Christianity, in this district. He is commemorated on November 2nd, in the Calendar of the Cathedral of Aberdeen, as a Bishop who led an eremitical life in Rathen; and in an account of this parish, by James Ogilvie, of Auchiries, contained in one of the volumes published by the Spaldng Club, it is said that a hollow, on the east side of Mormond, where he was supposed to have had his hermitage, was still com-

* Preface to the Book of Deer, p. iv.
* Dr James Robertson, Proc. Soc. Ant., Scot. II., 15.

monly known as St. Eddran's Slack.   Since that time, however, the name has quite died out of the recollection of the country people ; but I find, in an old map, of date 1774, a reference made to St. Edward's How, which appears by collation with some of the family papers, to be a miscalling of the name in question.

The Church of the Scots and Picts—agreeing, in general, with that of Ireland—differed in various points from those Churches of the west, which held to the See of Rome ; and among others, of course, from that founded by St. Augustine, in England, on the conversion of the Pagan Saxons, who had subverted the older Christianity of the provincial Britons.   The two Churches were, after a time, brought into collision by the large share which the Clergy, from Iona took in the conversion of the Saxons of Northumberland ; and owing to the commanding position they held there, the celebrated Conference of Whitby was convoked to adjust the claims of the rival missionaries.   Here the King, Oswy, gave in his adhesion to the Roman party, either from the real force of Wilfred's arguments on that side, or from the impression that his was the rising cause ; whereon the Celtic Clergy, who were unwilling to give up their peculiar usages, mostly withdrew, leaving the field to their opponents, and from that time, the Latin Christianity of St. Augustine's followers gradually prevailed over the whole Island south of the Forth.   The differences, so hotly contested, were in some points, as we should now think, quite trivial—as the fashion of the clerical tonsure and the time of keeping Easter, but the latter involved not only the Paschal solemnity itself, but also the precursory Lenten Fast, then very strictly kept ; and the festivals that followed, extending in all, over a full third of the year, and occupying a much more prominent place in the social usages of that age, than of the present day—while both the points in dispute were probably regarded primarily as symbols of national independence.

There seems also to have been this speciality among the Celts that the ecclesiastical jurisdiction lay with the heads of the religious houses, who, as a rule, were only presbyters, for though we find frequent mention of bishops, they do not appear to have had any proper dioceses or territorial rule, the office being retained mainly for the purpose of ordination, and being probably often conferred as a mark of respect on persons leading a hermit life, or otherwise regarded as of distinguished sanctity. Of such bishops, "unattached," we have numerous legends in the Aberdeen Breviary—St. Nathalan of Tulloch, St. Manire of Crathie, St. Ternan of Upper, and St· Devenick of Lower Banchory, St. Machar of Aberdeen, St. Moluac of Mortlach, St. Marnoch of Aberchirder, and St. Ethernan of Rathen, being instances in this part of Scotland. This Celtic speciality of vesting clerical rule in presbyter abbots has been ascribed to the respect paid to the memory of their apostle S. Columba who himself held that position, but a similar state of matters, in regard at least to the existence of numerous bishops without dioceses, prevailed also to some extent in Ireland, notwithstanding the admitted episcopal character of St. Patrick, and his successors in the primatial see of Armagh.

Eventually we find that the Celtic churches conformed in all particulars to the customs of the Church of Rome, as they prevailed in the southern part of the Island—moved thereto partly perhaps by

3

conviction, and partly by the force of circumstances. The example was set by Adamnan, one of the most illustrious successors of Columba in the Abbey of Iona, who in the year 704 (A.D.) adopted the Roman rule for the celebration of Easter, but as he died very soon after, the old usage held sway among the monks till 716, when they yielded to the persuations of Egbert, a Saxon brother, who had come to reside among them.

In the case of the Picts again—as formerly in Northumberland— the change was effected more by political influence, Nectan the king declaring for the Roman usages in 710, moved thereto—ostensibly at least—by a letter from the Abbot of Wearmouth, the composition possibly of the venerable Bede, who was then a monk in that house, and who gives the text at length in his Ecclesiastical History. The king's decision was probably but a prelude to the adoption of a policy which had for its object to transfer the Pictish people from the Columban to the Anglo-Roman communion, for in 717 Nectan is recorded to have driven out of his territory the Columban clergy— "the Family of Iona"—and it is not probable that the Island Church ever recovered its metropolitan jurisdiction during the continuance of the Pictish kingdom.

The presence of these refugees in the Scottish territory probably aggravated the disputes between the rival races of North Britain, and helped on the final rupture which resulted in the conquest of Pictland by Kenneth MacAlpin, the king of the Scots, in 843. In the face of the strong traditions of its exterminating character, we cannot well suppose this conquest was effected without much bloodshed, though it may have been worked out by policy as well as by force of arms;

for Kenneth had some claim, through the female line, to the Pictish throne, and was probably well supported by the Columban clergy whom it had been the policy of the Pictish kings to depress and hold in subjection. These princes having no metropolitan of their own, and being therefore exposed to claims both from Iona and York, were probably inclined so to hold the balance of power between these sees, as to secure in practice their own supremacy.

The Picts—if not destroyed—eventually lost their name, language, and entire nationality, for the conquerers gave their own designation to their new territory on the east coast, and the name of Scotland, hitherto confined to the country we now call Ireland, and the Dalriadic district of North Britain colonized from it, came henceforward to be extended to the whole of the latter country, and eventually to be applied to it alone—a change of designation which has proved a copious source of confusion in the history of those times. Concomitantly we find. the Pictish form of Celtic giving place to the Irish dialect, represented by the modern Gaelic, traces of the former remaining only in names of places—such as those in which the prefix *Aber* (so common in Wales) occasionally occurs along the East coast ; though even there it is more commonly superseded by the Gaelic *Inver.** A little later we find, at the time of the entries in the Book

---

* So entire has been the disappearance of Pictish—one of the four tongues in which the Gospel was preached in the time of Bede (Eccl. Hist. i. 1, iii. 7), that our conceptions of its affinities are mostly conjectural, but from such traces as can be picked up, Mr. Skene arrives at the conclusion that it was a *low* form of Gaelic, differing from it much as Dutch does from German, and to some extent approaching the Cymbric or Welsh (Pref. to Ancient Books of Wales). This might be due in part to intermixture of the race with refugees from South Britain.

of Deer, Irish or Gaelic had become the generally prevailing language of North Britain.

The union of the Scots and Picts was soon followed by the removal of the ecclesiastical primacy from Iona to Dunkeld, less, it would seem, from any political reason than from the fear of the Scandinavian rovers, who had already more than once pillaged the Holy Isle, murdering the abbot and monks, and dispersing the community. These savage forays of the heathen pirates of the North, which are almost the only events of the time that have come down to us, must have been in Scotland, as we know they were elsewhere, most prejudicial to civilization and settled government. Though the primary object of the pirates was plunder, in some cases they seem to have settled down in the country like the Anglo-Saxons in South Britain and the Normans in France. From the analogy between our patois and that of Northumberland and Yorkshire, it has been surmised that an Anglian, Frisian, or Danish settlement took place in Aberdeenshire, and to this the dedication of the old Church of Cruden to S. Olaus, the first Christian king of Norway, has been referred. But our historians ascribe this to a compact made on the occasion between Malcolm II., king of Scotland, and Sueno, king of Denmark, and represent the Danes as defeated, and either slaughtered or expelled, both at Cruden and Gamrie. At Memsie, in Rathen, the cairns indicate some great battle, but whether referable or not to the same contest it is impossible to say. The dedication, however, of Cruden to a Scandinavian saint is certainly more suggestive of the successful establishment of the invaders on the coast, than of their defeat and expulsion.

In 907 the primacy was shifted again to St. Andrew's, and an important step taken towards the establishment of the diocesan system by the erection of that church into a regular episcopal see. A church indeed seems to have been founded at St. Andrew's about a century before, by Hungus, king of the Picts, though subsequently secularized, as was the case with so many of the Celtic religious houses. One cause, no doubt, of the decadence of Christianity among the Celts was this extensive secularization, fostered as it was by the isolation of the national church, which thus failed to supply any corrective to the abuse from the influence of other parts of Christendom. The evil, however, seems to have been less prevalent in Buchan—in the case of Deer, at least, we have evidence from the entries in the volume quoted of numerous gifts to St. Drostan's House, extending on to the middle of the 12th century; though the concluding charter granted by King David shows that eventually, even here, the religious foundation was threatened with such encroachments as rendered needful an appeal to the royal authority, founded on the memoranda of the previous donations preserved in the marginal notes in their church books.

But whatever local exceptions may be admitted, the general decline of earnestness indicated by the secularization of church property seems to have gone on progressively till the time of Malcolm Canmore, when, if we may trust the accounts of Turgot, the adviser and biographer of his wife, the Saxon princess Margaret, vital Christianity in Scotland was at a very low ebb, the observance of sunday and the use of the sacraments had fallen into great neglect, marriages within the prohibited degrees were not uncommon, and many barbarous superstitions had crept into the services of the church.

Hence we find, as was but natural, that as soon as the reforming zeal of the queen began to fan the dull embers of religion among her Celtic subjects, the process of assimilation to the Latinized Christianity of the English Church, in which she had herself been trained, went on *pari passu* with the removal of the old standing abuses, and the promotion of piety and learning among the clergy. The work was consummated by her son David (also of English training), to whom we owe the establishment of the later Scottish sees, and the translation to Aberdeen of the bishoprick founded by his father at Mortlach, in 1063.

To the erection of proper dioceses, succeeded that of territorial parishes, a sequence indeed to be observed over the greater part of Christendom, though in some regions of the East, the idea seems never yet to have suggested itself of mapping out the country into smaller sections or parishes, to promote the pastoral efficiency of the clergy, as the division into the larger districts or dioceses subserves the good government of the church at large, but the evangelizing of the general population is still left, as in the old Celtic times among ourselves, to the missionary labours of the staff of clergy attached to the larger churches, whether Cathedral, Collegiate, or Monastic. In this establishment of the parochial system in Scotland, the smaller monasteries—many of which, doubtless, were in a very decaying state—were replaced by parish churches, if indeed the former were not actually converted into the latter.

As the revival of religion—inaugurated by Margaret, and zealously followed up afterwards by David I.—told gradually on the country at large, we find that offerings began anew to be made for ecclesiastical foundations, though now of a different type. The new English settlers of Norman descent appear the foremost in this good work. Thus, in the year 1219, William Comyn, or Cumine, Earl of Buchan, and maternal grandson of Colban, the last granter recorded in the book of Deer, founded at a spot about two miles west of the parish church, which had replaced St. Drostan's Monastery, an Abbey of Cistercian Monks, from Kinloss, on the Findhorn—Alexander, the prior, being the first superior; and the Abbot of Kinloss, the visitor of the new foundation. No trace of the original charter has been discovered, but it seems to have conveyed, among other possessions, the parish Church, with the lands which had belonged to the old monastery.

The turn of affairs, after the war of independence, led to the proscription and eventual extinction of the Cumines, who, as Earls of Buchan, represented, through the female line, the old Celtic chiefs of the district, but who, by their espousal of the English cause, were among the most formidable opponents of Bruce, and were farther embittered against him by the personal feud originating in the murder of the Red Cumine, at Dumfries. On their ruin arose the family of the Cheynes, of Inverugie, who, adhering latterly to the fortunes of Bruce, remained in possession of their lands in Buchan, besides others granted in Caithness and elsewhere; but soon after, the male line becoming extinct, their possessions passed by marriage, mainly to the Marischal Family, which continued the leading house in Buchan till after the middle of the 17th century.

As the increase of ecclesiastical abuses progressed, which was the immediate cause of the overthrow of the old religion at the time of the Reformation, the same secularization of Church property occurred which marked the decline of the Celtic institutions. Thus, in the year 1543, the fourth Earl Marischal got his brother Robert appointed Abbot of Deer while still a minor; and on his death eight years after, his own son, Robert, then only fifteen years of age. The latter, in 1587, resigned all the monastic property into the king's hands, to be erected into the temporal barony of Altrie, in favour of himself, and after his death, of his nephew, George, sixth Earl Marischal, and his heirs male. Who can wonder that the ardent Montalembert, in contrasting the aggrandisement of the House of Marischal by the seizure of church property at this time with the expatriation and eventual extinction of the family which followed at no distant period, should see in their fall the fulfilment of the saying of Columba, who, in his parting blessing to his infant foundation, left, as his word, that "whosoever should come against it, should not be many yeared or victorious?"

Elsewhere in this district, the great social convulsion of the Reformation left comparatively small traces of the kind. There were no other rich foundations to tempt the cupidity of the nobles; and though the parish churches were doubtless impoverished for the time, yet, by the restoration of the teinds under Charles I., their financial position was probably rendered, in most respects, better than before.

In this cursory survey of the introduction and early progress of Christianity in our quarter, I regret to have had to omit all reference to the origin and early history of most of the parishes of our district. Want of time, however, besides other cogent reasons, put it out of my power to enter on the consideration of this subject at present.

Early Progress of Christianity in Buchan.

PART II.

On the Origin of the Parish Churches in the District of Deer.

THE allusion, at the close of a former paper, to the interesting subject of the origin of our Parish Churches, as it led to the members of the club expressing a wish for the farther examination of the question, has, I fear, raised expectations which it is impossible to fulfil, owing to the almost absolute deficiency of materials. This makes it necessary to preface the present communication with a sort of apology for the fragmentary character of the notices contained in it. When we consider the importance and real magnitude of the parochial arrangement, we may well wonder that we have no record of its commencement and progress, and that it is but very rarely we can assign a date with any distinctness to the foundation of one of the older parishes, or indeed to the erection of the older existing churches. All we can find, in general, is a notice at some early date of such a parish as already in existence, by a record of a presentation to the charge—a benefaction to the living ; or, it may be, the signature of the parson as a witness to some deed. There is, no doubt, a more than ordinary obscurity about the old church history of Scotland ; but, to some extent, there is a like deficiency of information about the origin of parishes in England and other parts of Christendom, in which the system has long been in full operation. This is probably, in part, due to the arrangement being brought in, not by any general or authoritative action, but as it were by a process of spontaneous development—churches being first founded by individuals in the more important localities, and only acquiring a territorial jurisdiction from becoming naturally the resort of the population of the district.

If the public authorities came in at all, it was probably not till a period subsequent to the virtual establishment of the older and more important parishes, and in the way of completing the system by settling more definitively the boundaries of such as were already formed, and, perhaps, carrying out the same arrangement in the less thickly peopled districts to which it had not yet extended. We find an indication, at least, of such a state of transition between the first formation of parishes and their systematic allocation throughout the land, in the chapels which occur here and there distinct from the parish churches, and which seem to have been a sort of mission stations, served by clerics from some of the religious houses, or larger parish churches in the neighbourhood. As examples may be mentioned, those at Fetter-Angus, Kinninmonth, and Chapelton, near Fraserburgh ; and in some other parts of the country, the ruins or sites of such churches are more numerous than here.

The rise of the parochial system in Scotland probably followed as the natural result of the influx of settlers from England, which began before the time of Malcolm Canmore, but was especially fostered by David, who had spent so much of his early life in that country; and the first traces we find of it are in the southern counties. From these it gradually spread northwards during the long period of amity between the two kingdoms, which preceded the war of independence.

There were, no doubt, many cases in Scotland like the instance given by Professor Innes, in the parish of Ednam,* in which a settler from England, coming into the possession of land by grant, or purchase, built a church for the benefit of his barony, and endowed it with the tithes of the produce. But in the older Celtic settlements sacred edifices had existed for many generations—not on the parochial footing, but as clan churches—erected originally by, or in memory of, the first preachers, for the use of the tribe at the time of its conversion; the building being kept up, and the priest supported by landed endowments, or by the voluntary contributions of the clansmen, paid mostly in labour and in kind, but without any assessment of the nature of tithes, of which no trace is to be found in the early polity of the country. All the old Celtic Saints were great church builders—even such as did not settle down permanently in one spot tarried at different stations, as they went on their preaching tours—erecting churches as memorials of their visit, and a means of binding their converts together in the profession of the Christian faith; and when they travelled in company, they added to them monastic buildings, to be tenanted by some of the

* Sketches of Early Scottish History, p. 11.

band, who were left to carry on the work. To Columba himself tradition ascribes the foundation of 300 churches—half in Ireland and as many in Scotland. Modern learning, says Montalembert, has registered the existence of ninety, whose origin goes back to his day, and traces still remain of thirty-two in the country of the Scots, in the west, while twenty-one mark the principal stations of the great missionary in the land of the Picts.* " If a notable conversion was effected, if the preacher had, or believed he had, some direct and sensible encouragement from heaven, a chapel was the fitting memorial of the event. Wherever a hopeful congregation was assembled, a place of worship was required. When a saintly pastor died, his grateful flock dedicated a church to his memory."†

Of course, it is not to be supposed that the edifices were such as we now use for public worship. There was probably not one stone building among all those founded by S. Columba in the mainland of Scotland, though some small dome-shaped cells of stonework, in the Western Isles, are referred to that age; in general, they were, like the houses, humble structures of wood or wattles. Even in Iona, the monastic buildings appear to have been of wattle-work, and the church of wood, with perhaps the altar of stone. In numerous spots over Argyleshire and the Western Isles, where sculptured stones and crosses now exist in profusion, but where there are no remains of a stone building, we may presume that the church,

* Monks of the West, III., 161. He refers no doubt to the list of Columban foundations, given by Dr. Reeves, in his edition of Adamnan's Life of the Saint—" Churches either which were founded by S. Columba, or in which his memory was specially venerated" —a list which by no means pretends to be a complete enumeration.

† Innes' Sketches of Early Scottish History, p. 2.

round which they clustered, was built of timber or wattles.* Stone buildings were for long so rare as to acquire a name, nearly as lasting in their own neighbourhood as the famous *Candida Casa* of S. Ninian, in Galloway. Thus, on Deeside, we have the two Banchories, or "fair choirs" of S. Ternan and S. Devenick, and in this district there is the Church of Tyrie, styled in history the "White Kirk of Buchan," and known even still by the older inhabitants of the parish, as "the White Kirk on the Green Hill."

The conversion of these clan chapels into parish churches, supported by an assessment of tithes, was probably a change as gradual as the substitution of stone buildings for the original wigwams, and was effected more by the change of feeling which replaced the clannish usages with the feudal and hierarchical institutions, than by any official or legislative act.

Here two points of enquiry present themselves in connection with the subject before us :

1. The origin of the older churches which preceded the formation of parishes, but determined, in so far, their situation.

2. The establishment of parishes on the footing they hold in our later ecclesiastical history.

On the latter point I have really nothing to say beyond the few remarks I have made already, unless in regard to those exceptional cases, in which additional parishes were formed after the general movement in this direction was over, and when their organization—

* Burton's History, I., 266.

involving certain legal formalities—has, in consequence, come to be entered on record.

New parishes were formed in this way by the subdivision of the older. Thus S. Nicholas was formed out of that of S. Machar, as the burghal parish for the increasing population of the town of Aberdeen. In 1288 the Knights Templars obtained the erection of an independent chapel dedicated to S. Mary, for their lands in Culter on the river Dee, which cut them off more or less from the parish church of S. Peter, and the chapelry afterwards became the parish of Mary Culter.* Glenbucket also was separated from Logie Mar by a commission of the bishop issued in consequence of some people of the glen, on their way to the parish church at Easter tide, being caught in a storm in which five or six of them perished. But such cases were exceptional, and the parishes mostly continued as originally constituted till the Reformation, when many were so dilapidated, in the poorer parts of the country, as to bring about their suppression or conjunction with others. Somewhat later, a revival took place in certain districts, and new parishes were made to meet the increase of population, mainly it would seem at the instance of Bishop Patrick Forbes, who of all the prelates of the later Scottish Church, probably was the most liberal patron of learning, as well as the greatest church builder. At this time were formed most of the later parishes in Buchan, viz., New Deer, Strichen, Longside, and Pitsligo; and many old churches were rebuilt, not, it must be admitted, in the best style. Udny was erected before this time under Bishop Blackburn in 1605.

* Professor Innes' Early Scottish History, 14.

New Machar dates from 1618? Newhills from 1662, and Monquhitter from 1640.

The first rise of parishes seems to have coincided with the extinction of the old religious houses, and in some cases was probably taken advantage of for the suppression of these obstructive institutions, the monastic being converted into the parish church, and the resumption of the revenues by the lay patron perhaps connived at, in consideration of his payment of tithes to the parochial clergy, a custom which does not appear to have had any place in the Celtic polity. "Thus"— as the Editor of the Book of Deer observes—"the monastery of Mortlach with its dependency of Clova continued to flourish till the time of David I., when both reappear in record as churches of districts. The monastery of S. Congan at Turriff became the church of the parish of that name, and the House of S. Drostan at Deer, now disappeared in like manner in the parochial arrangement of the country; while in both cases the lands of these monastries seem to have been resumed by the Earls of Buchan, the representatives of the earlier Mormaers."*

* Book of Deer, Pref., p. ix. The old Celtic monastery of S. Congan at Turriff, above referred to, is known only by the mention of two of its officials as witnesses to grants in the Book of Deer, viz., Cormac the Abbot, in the reign of David I., and Domongart the Ferleginn—an officer who (at least in the Irish monasteries) superintended the conventual school and had charge of the manuscripts. As is the case at Mortlach which is dedicated to a S. Molocus or Mó-luak, so here also, we have no evidence of the actual foundation of the house by the saint whose name it bears, for Congan an ascetic in the beginning of the eighth century, seems to have spent his life even more exclusively than Mo-luak in the West of Scotland. In the Aberdeen Breviary he is mentioned as an Irish chief, who leaving Leinster, his native country, with his sister Kentigerna, her three sons Felan, Fursey, and Ultan, and seven other clerics, settled at Loch Alsh in Argyleshire, where a church was afterwards built in his honour by his nephew S. Felan. Before the time of Alexander II., the monastery had given place to a parish church, and a reference to *the monk's gate*, in the

The other question—that of the origin of the older churches, which became in course of time the nuclei of parishes—though also one of great obscurity, still admits of a certain amount of elucidation, though the results we can arrive at are generally very indefinite, and in most instances largely conjectural; and in no case can they be considered as applying to the fabrics which have come down to our day, even in the most ruinous condition, but only to the first erection in the same places of some building, however provisional, for the celebration of Divine Service.

Some general idea may be formed of the relative antiquity of our country churches, by attending to the names of the saints which they bear. As a rule the oldest dedications are to Celtic Saints. It seems to be a general principle, that in all parts of Christendom, the devotion of the common people was most marked to those whose personal labours and self-denying life had first gained their affections, and whose courageous testimony to the verities they preached, and resistance to the death of all attempts to seduce them from their allegiance to their Divine Master, had brought them over to a system of faith and worship, that took a deeper hold of human nature than any of the old idolatries.

Now, in this part of Scotland at least, the first missionaries were

foundation deed of an alms-house at Turriff, by William, Earl of Buchan, in 1273, is the only farther indication we find of its previous existence. In the ruins of the old parish church of Turriff, a remarkable fresco was lately discovered of S. Ninian, habited as a bishop, with his right hand raised in benediction, and with the pastoral staff in his left. Dr. Stuart gives good reasons for believing that this was but one of a series of similar paintings round the Church, executed by Andrew Bairham, an artist engaged by the Abbot of Kinloss in 1538, about which time the Choir was rebuilt by Alexander Lyon, a son of the fourth Lord Glammis, the chanter of Moray and parson of Turriff. Book of Deer, Pref., p. cxlii.

all of Celtic extraction—schooled in S. Columba's famous monastery of Iona. Hence an anterior probability in favour of the greater anti- quity of such churches as that of S. Colm's at Lonmay—S. Drostan's at Aberdour and Deer—S. Ethernan's at Rathen—S. Modan's at Philorth, and S. Fergus' near Peterhead—a probability which falls in completely with the testimony, such as it is, of the ecclesiastical and traditionary legends, and is farther corroborated by other kinds of evidence, both internal and external, such as is brought forward in the Book of Deer in illustration of the visit of S. Columba to the district, and his committal of the superiority of the religious house founded at Deer to his disciple S. Drostan—or again, of the story of the missions of S. Fergus to various parts of the country, and of his labours in particular in that district on the lower Ugie, which still bears his name.

To these points, which I mentioned in my former paper, I need not again recur, but I may add one or two particulars in regard to the traditionary founder of Rathen—who is commemorated in the Aber- deen Calendar on Dec. 2, under the name of Ethernanus, and described as a Bishop who led a hermitical life in that parish. His proper name was probably Ernan, which, in the local dialect has become Eddran. Some authors make Ernan or Ethernan a nephew of S. Columba. It is known that the Saint had relatives of that name—both an uncle and a nephew—but neither of them are ever styled bishops. The name in fact was then very common. Dr. Reeves, in the notes to his edition of Adamnan's life of S. Columba, says there are twenty-six in the Irish Calendar—and some of them, like our Buchan Saint, appear under various guises, such as *Marnan* and *Marnoch*—said to be abbreviations of *Mo-ernan* and *Mo-ernan-oc*—in which the prefix and suffix are expressive of affectionate familiarity (my little Ernan). So modified, the name appears *locally* in Kilmarnock and Inchmarnock, and *personally* in Marnan, a Saint whose head is said, in an old martyrology,* to have been preserved as a relic in a church dedicated to his memory at Aberchirder, in the parish of Marnoch, in Banffshire. Cairnmurnan, in the parish of Tyrie, in closer proximity to the scene of S. Ethernan's labours, presents us with another example probably of the same name, which is connected also with the copious fountain in the glen below, known as "The Murnan Well," one of the sources of the water of Rathen. If the Hermit of Mormond came forth from S. Columba's first settlement on the coast, this spring might well mark a station in his course, as it lies in the natural line of transit from Aberdour to Rathen; but there is no legend so far as I know bearing on the point, and the name may after all be rather a descriptive one.†

Of the patron of Philorth we have only this notice in the Aberdeen Breviary on Nov. 14, "*Modanus Episcopus et Confessor qui apud Philorth percelebris habetur,*" but Dempster calls Modan an abbot in Buchan, and adds that his own contemporary, John Fraser (a cadet of Philorth, and successively Professor and Rector of the University of Paris) had his "Acts" in MS. and intended to publish them, but was prevented by death. S. Modan may have been connected with S. Drostan's house at Aberdour, for the name crops up in *Auchmedden*

---

* Given in the Index Volume of the Proceedings of the Scottish Society of Antiquaries, p. 361.

† Cairn Murnan = Mount Pleasant, according to the ingenious suggestion of a friend.

—S. Modan's field—in that neighbourhood. But we find it also in *Pitmedden* on Donside, and again in Udny, and of old the intermediate parish of Fintray seems to have been dedicated to S. Modan (though at a later period it was rather connected with the name of S. Giles), for in the New Statistical Account of Scotland, the minister states that he " has in his possession a silver cup, belonging to the parish, bearing date 1632, which tradition says was formed from a silver head of S. Meddan, the titular saint of the parish "—probably a silver reliquary or case containing the skull—"which, in days of popish superstition, was wont to be carried through the parish in procession, for the purpose of bringing down rain, or clearing up the weather, as circumstances might require." There is another S. Modan, an abbot, commemorated Feb. 4, but he seems to have been connected with Falkirk and other localities in the south of Scotland. Distinct from both, probably, is Middanus, commemorated by Camerarius on April 29, whom Bishop Forbes thinks may probably be that S. Medan of Airlie, whose " bell " was still held in reverence in 1447, when it was given as part of the dowry of the wife of Sir John Ogilvy of Lentrethyn, though within the present century the same relic was sold as a bit of old iron.*

Next to the Celtic dedications are probably to be put those to St. Peter, which are not uncommon in some parts of Scotland, though Peterhead is the only case in our own neighbourhood. The reason for assigning this position to these dedications is Bede's account of Abbot Ceolfrid's embassy to the Pictish king, which, though I have already made reference to it in my former paper, it will be advisable

* Scottish Calendars, p. 399.

now to state in the historian's own words, in order to bring out its bearing on this point. "About the year 710, Nectan, king of the Picts who inhabit the northern regions of Britain, renounced the error in which he and his people had been involved concerning Easter. To bring his subjects more readily to the right observance, he sent deputies to Ceolfrid, Abbot of Wearmouth, in Northumberland, desiring he would send him a letter of instruction on this subject and the tonsure of the clergy. Moreover, he requested that architects might be sent to build a church of stone after the fashion of the Romans, promising it should be dedicated in honour of St. Peter." The Abbot, assenting to his requests, sent the architects he asked for, and also a long letter on the points in question, which Bede gives in full, being himself, very possibly, its real author. The letter was read before a council of the nobility and prelates of the Picts, and at its close, the king, declaring himself fully convinced by its arguments, proceeded at once to enforce the Roman usages as to the observance of Easter and the tonsure; "and the nation," continues Bede, "thus reformed, rejoiced that it was subjected, as it were anew, to the direction of Peter, the most blessed chief of the Apostles, and that it was to be protected by his patronage." * Hence there is some ground for referring these foundations approximately to the early part of the eighth century.

On somewhat similar grounds we should put after the foregoing churches dedicated to S. Andrew, of which also we have but one example in the district, that of Tyrie. The adoption by our forefathers of S. Andrew, as their titular saint, dates from about the

* Bede's History of the English Nation, Book V., 21.

middle of the eighth century, and is associated with the legend of the translation of his relics from Patras, in Asia Minor, to the capital of Fife. Mr. Skene has lately shown, in a very ingenious paper in the 4th volume of the proceedings of the Scottish Society of Antiquaries, that there is good reason for considering the translation to S. Andrews of the reputed relics of the Apostle as a historical fact, which he would refer to the reign of the Pictish king, Angus I., A.D. 732, and he gives plausible ground for holding that their immediate source was neither Patras in Greece—the scene of the Apostle's martyrdom, as reported in one legend, nor Constantinople, where they were carried by the Emperor Constantine, as we are told in another—but Hexham in Northumberland, to which we know that Bishop Acca or some of his predecessors had brought reputed relics of S. Andrew from Rome or Gaul. Acca, being driven away from his see in 732, took refuge among the Picts, and Mr. Skene suggests that his taking with him the relics, and depositing them at the place in Fife, now called after the Apostle's name, may have given rise to the legend. That such a translation took place from some quarter is probable, both from the circumstantial character of the narrative, and from certain coincidences with other recorded facts; such as the expedition against the Scots of Argyle, in returning from which the king met the deputation bearing the relics, at Kindrochet, in Braemar, where a church was afterwards built in honour of S. Andrew.[*]

The principal difficulty is about Regulus, the chief character in the legend. The voyage from Patras or Constantinople may be

---

[*] The Early Ecclesiastical Settlements at St. Andrews, Proceedings of the Scottish Society of Antiquaries, IV., p. 301.

thrown overboard, with all its supernatural decorations, and a strong case appears to be made out for Hexham, but if we are to give up as " unhistorical " the time-honoured name of S. Rule, what have we to say in support of the real existence of almost any of our other local saints ? This difficulty Mr. Skene admits, and, in explanation, he offers the conjecture that Regulus, Bishop of Senlis in Gaul, who was originally from Greece, and lived in the fourth century, may have been the person who took away the relics from Patras or Constantinople, as he is commemorated on March 30, the day on which the Aberdeen Breviary gives the legend of S. Rule. If Acca at a later age brought the relics from his church to Hexham, and from that to S. Andrews, he might also have brought the legend of their translation from Greece by S. Regulus. The usual day assigned to S. Regulus or S. Rule in Scotland is 17th Oct., and as this is the commemoration in the Irish Calendar of S. Regulus or Riaguil of Muicinei on Loch Derg, Mr. Skene thinks the Irish saint, though he had really no connection with Scotland, has fallen heir to the reverence paid to the Greek monk, as the legendary bearer of the relics of S. Andrew.

- To these fragmentary notices, which are all I have been able to collect on the subject in question, I will add, in conclusion, only a few remarks on the grouping of the parishes into ecclesiastical districts. As the division of Scotland into dioceses preceded the origin of parishes, all the latter in this quarter of course belonged, as soon as constituted, to the diocese of Aberdeen, which, in geographical extent, very nearly covered the north-east district, between the rivers Dee and Spey, as it included the whole county of Aberdeen, except

Strathbogie, and about one-half of the county of Banff. The province of Buchan had under its old chiefs or maormaers, and later, under its earls, a recognized political status, which was afterwards merged in the sheriffdom or shire of Aberdeen, but ecclesiastically, even after the latter had come to represent, in a general way, the diocese of Aberdeen, Buchan still appears as one of its component deaneries. The first division we find recorded is into the three deaneries of Mar, Buchan, and Garioch, the latter lying between the upper or western corners of the others. To these were afterwards added Aberdeen, to which were transferred the lower parishes of Mar, and the Boyne, including those in the lower part of Banff and the north coast of Aberdeenshire adjoining. By this later arrangement, Tyrie, Aberdour, and nine other parishes to the west, were transferred from the deanery of Buchan to that of the Boyne.

After the Reformation, the first notice we find of change is the proposal submitted to the General Assembly of Glasgow, in 1551, to divide the diocese of Aberdeen into the synods of Aberdeen and Banff—the former to consist of the presbyteries of Aberdeen, Inverurie, and Kincardine O'Neil—the latter of those of Banff, Deer, and Kildrummie—but this scheme does not seem to have taken effect at the time, and it was not till 1584 that the division into presbyteries was fully established. By the scheme then adopted, the diocese was divided into five presbyteries, Aberdeen, Inverurie, Kincardine, Banff, and Deer, which were to form two synods, one meeting at Aberdeen, the other at Turriff. When the two were united is not ascertained, but it was ordered by the General Assembly of Glasgow in 1638 that the Provincial Synod of Aberdeen should consist of the presbyteries of Aberdeen, Kincardine, Alford, Garioch, Ellon, Deer, Turriff, and Fordyce ; and this has since been adhered to, under episcopal as well as presbyterian rule, except during some years after the establishment of the latter in 1690, when all the presbyterian ministers, being very few, formed but one united pres-bytery. In 1697, their number being increased to 15, they divided themselves into three, after which the old number of eight, was gradually, and in no long time, restored.*

I conclude with the few scraps of information I have been able to pick up in regard to the several parishes in this quarter. Two-thirds were certainly constituted at a very early period, though I do not see that we can assign a more precise date than the interval of a century and a-half, between the reign of David I. and that of his descendant, Alex. III., who was killed in 1285. We find them pretty much on their present footing in the "Taxatio ecclesiarum et beneficiarum per episcopatum Aberdonense," which is referred by Dr. Joseph Robert-son to the year 1366, and individual notices occur of yet earlier date. Thus we find from the Ragman Roll (p. 164) that Andrew, parson of the church of Philorth swore fealty to Edward I. in the year 1296,† and in a roll of missing charters of Robert I., there is one referring to the patronage of the Church of Philorth, of date 1330. In the troubled interval between this and the extinction of the old dynasty we can hardly suppose anything to have been done in the way of parochial organization.

The ancient parishes I may take alphabetically, though in regard

* View of Diocese of Aberdeen, p. 223, note.
† Pratt's Buchan, Appendix II.

6

to the first in order—as also probably in date—Aberdour, I have
hardly anything more to say. Of the old church, now in ruins, the
writer in the Statistical Account of Scotland, observes that the aisle
was rebuilt about 1764, "and the steeple" (of which no trace now remains), he continues, "was rebuilt some years after." The modern
building in the village of New Aberdour, dates from 1818. Aberdour
figures in the ballad of Hardiknute, the antiquity of which has been
successfully vindicated by Mr. Clyne, who gives good grounds also for
considering the Buchan Station, and not that on the Frith of Forth
to be the Aberdour there commemorated.

CRIMOND I find is called Retref (Rattray) in the *Taxatio*, before
quoted, and possibly the original parish church may be represented
by the ruined chapel—founded, it is said, in memory of a son
of one of the old Earls of Buchan (Cumine) who was drowned in a
well there. On a neighbouring eminence, called the Castle Hill, is
said to have been a chief seat of that family, and round the church
there grew up a little town, which was erected into a Royal Burgh by
Queen Mary, in 1563, to put a stop to a dispute between the Earls
Marischal and Erroll about the superiority. At that time the Loch
of Strathbeg was represented by a small estuary, navigable by boats,
where the water of Rattray fell into the sea—this being silted up in
the end of the seventeenth century, the stream overflowed, and gave
rise to the present freshwater lake. But even before this the town
had decayed, probably from the shoaling of the harbour, and the rise
of Peterhead and Fraserburgh on either side, for Robert Gordon of
Straloch, in 1651, speaks of the *remains* of the town; and Keith, in

1727, says it consisted of but nine or ten houses,* now I believe reduced to one.   The present church in the village of Crimond is stated
to have been built in 1812, to replace an older structure supposed to
date from 1576—"at least," says the Statistical Account, " this date
is above one of the doors ; it is probable, however, it had only been
repaired in that year, as there is still a font stone in the east end."
It is hardly necessary to observe that in Catholic Churches the font
properly stands in the *west* end, and is never built into the wall—
what is meant here is no doubt a *piscina* or drain for rinsing the
sacramental vessels, and its presence is a pretty clear evidence of
pre-reformation date.

DEER—The date of the foundation of the Abbey is 1219, but
Dr. Stuart gives good reasons for believing that a parish church
existed here before then, and it is confirmatory of this, that it never
was subject to the Abbey.   The present building—dating from 1788
or 1789—occupies the site of the body of the older edifice, but some
fragments of a former church, in the pointed style, still remain at the
east end.

Along with ST. FERGUS or Longley, I will take also PETERHEAD,
as I think there is some probability that when the former first became
a parish, it included the country on both sides of the Ugie—St.
Peter's Church being originally but a chapel for one part of the
district, and acquiring a proper parochial status only at a late

* View of Diocese of Aberdeen.

period, in consequence perhaps of some jealousy between the Marischal Family and the Cheynes of Inverugie. The old name of the parish of Peterhead—*Inverugie Petri* or *Peterugie* (that is St. Peter's in Inverugie)—suggests such a connection, as in the somewhat analogous case before mentioned of the dissociation of Peter Culter and Mary Culter on Deeside. The change might have coincided with the erection of the old church to the south of the town, whose architecture indicates a more advanced style of building—if not a later date—than the ruins of most of the other ancient country churches. The town is of later growth—the charter of erection, in which it is called " Keith Inch, alias Peterhead," being from George, Earl Marischal in 1593. The modern parish church was built in 1803, to take the place of one erected in 1771; " on that piece of ground called the Little Links."* The old churchyard of St. Fergus in the Links of Inverugie is still the burying place of the parish. My recollection of its appearance about twenty-five years ago quite corresponds with the short description in Dr. Pratt's work on Buchan. " There are still to be seen fragments of the font, and some pieces of rude sculpture which had belonged to the old church. Part of the south wall, to the depth of several feet still remains, but completely covered [outside] by the accumulated soil. The area of the church which is still traceable, shows it to have been a long narrow building." The fragments of the font, which indicated an octagonal form, have now disappeared, and in the rebuilding of the enclosure and levelling of the ground, which was done about three years ago, the distinctness of the remaining portions of the church walls has been lost in the

* Minutes of Presbytery of Deer.

high stone fence surrounding the churchyard. Still, notwithstanding the glaze of the new mortar, and the strange assortment of modern monuments put up against the walls, there is something wonderfully striking in this little city of the dead set down in a wilderness of fantastic sand hills, and quite away from all habitations of the living. This aspect of the neighbourhood at present is probably due to the drifting of the sands; and the soil turned up making fresh graves gives clear indications of the original seats of the labours of St. Fergus having been on fertile land, and probably a chief centre of the population of the district at the time. In 1616 the Minutes of the Presbytery of Deer record the "transporting of the Kirk" to its present site, about two miles distant. A second church was built here in 1763, which was again replaced in 1869 by the present fabric.

LONMAY—The old church at the village of St. Colm's was given up in 1607, and one built in the present churchyard near Cairness. The existing building there dates from 1787.

PHILORTH—Of the date of the old church at Kirkton we have, as usual, no record. The church in Fraserburgh was first built by Alexander Fraser of Philorth, who succeeded his grandfather in 1569, and afterwards received the honour of knighthood from James VI., by whom he was much esteemed. Soon after his succession, we are told, he began to build a large and beautiful town at Faithlie, which had already been erected by a charter of Queen Mary into a Burgh of Barony. In 1570 he laid the foundation of the tower on Kinnaird's Head, and next year he built a church. In 1576 he began to build a harbour at the same place and, his ambition soaring always higher, he projected founding there also a completely developed university, for which he obtained a charter from the Crown and Parliament in 1592, with a further confirmation in 1601. The words of the latter are worth quoting: " Our Sovereign Lord and the three estates of Parliament understanding that Alexander Fraser of Fraserburgh·has obtained a new infeftment of his barony of Philorth, &c., in which also he has obtained the town and burgh of Faithlie—now called Fraserburgh—to be erected a free burgh of barony, with express liberty to erect a University, big and mak colleges, and place masters and teachers, with all the privileges and immunities that may pertain to a free University—since which time the said burgh has not only greatly flourished in bigging, repair, and resort of people, so that sundry gentry of the county are becoming inhabitants and burgesses of the said burgh, but also the said Alexander has made there an sure haven and port, and also being of deliberate mind and purpose to erect an University, has begun to edify and big up a college, which not only will tend to the great decorement of the country, but also to the advancement of the lost and tint youth, in bringing them up in learning and virtue, to the great honour and welfare of our Sovereign Lord and nation." The charter goes on to provide for the support of the officials of the college, by the mortification of the teinds and manses of Philorth, Tyrie, Rathen, and Crimond, under the patronage of Sir Alexander and his successors, the Professors enjoying these livings being bound also to conduct the pastoral duties of the parishes themselves, or to provide substitutes for the purpose. The college buildings were actually commenced, but the scheme seems to have miscarried in the end from some dispute with the Presbytery. From the imperfect evidence remaining there is reason to suspect that the principal named by the General Assembly—Fairholme, the minister of Fraserburgh, a rigid calvinist—was not acceptable to Sir Alexander. The present parish church was built in 1802, on the side of the former. In this parish there was also of old a small religious house, dependent on the Abbey of Deer.

RATHEN Church, lately dismantled, on the completion of the new handsome structure, is the only one in the district which has continued in use from before the Reformation to our own day. Like the old church of Aberdour it is distinguished by a south wing or transept opening at right angles into the body of the church, by a circular arch—taking the place apparently of the Lady chapel, which in most mediæval churches is added on at the east end of the chancel. Originally the floor, both of this wing and of the sanctuary, or east end of the body of the church, seems to have been on a higher level, and approached from the western part by one or two steps ; but at the time of the repairs executed after the Reformation, when all the walls appear to have been rebuilt, except those of the wing, and of the west gable of the church, it is probable that the floor of the main building was brought all to one level by excavating the eastern end, and that the floor of the wing was sloped down to meet it, for there is a marked incline from end to end of the latter, and in both the loose bones of old interments cropped up on the surface, among the feet of the worshippers, in a most unseemly manner. The date of these alterations is probably indicated by the figures, 1625, on a sundial on the end gable of the south wing. .

TYRIE—The present parish church was built in 1800. It appears from a notice of the former building in the Statistical Account that the earliest date found on the pews was 1596, and that since then it was twice repaired or partially rebuilt—in 1710 and 1773—but I am inclined to think that the present occupies the same site as the original structure, notwithstanding a vague tradition that the old ecclesiastical buildings were at Mains of Tyrie, where bones are said to have been turned up in trenching the garden. I find also an allusion in the statistical account to a tradition of a religious house in the neighbourhood of the present site. " The present church was built (as tradition says) for a chapel to a religious house in the vicinity, and had an aisle joined to it when it became a parish church." The old names, however, in the neighbourhood, as Kirkton and Kirkmyres, point to the present as the site of the church, if not from its first plantation, at least from a very early period. Tyrie, under its old name of the White Kirk of Buchan, is said to have been a noted place of pilgrimage, but the only historical fact I have met with about it is the appointment, as rector, of Hector Boece, the historian and first principal of the University of Aberdeen. He seems to have held the living only for a year or two before his death. It is not probable he was much in residence, but his account of the barnacle log kept in the church is suggestive of his having examined it personally. The log, he tells us, was washed ashore at Pitsligo, covered with barnacles, and when it was cut up by order of the lord of the place, is said to have been found full of worms, some of which had limbs in course of formation, while others had attained the perfect form of birds, both fledged and naked. The notion that barnacles gavé rise to a particular kind of geese was quite prevalent among naturalists at that time, suggested perhaps by a sort of resemblance which the tentacles of this shell-fish have to the sprouting feathers of a newly hatched bird. My grandfather, John Forbes of Boyndlie, I am told, believed that he had in his possession this identical piece of wood.

Of the post-reformation parishes, the first formed was LONGSIDE, where a church was built in 1619 or 1620, as a chapel of ease apparently to Petérugie (Peterhead). A separate parish was soon after formed for it, partly, it would seem, out of Crimond, but chiefly out of Peterugie, whence it was called at first New Peterugie, or more shortly, New Peter. The present parish church was built in 1835.

Next comes AUCHREDDIE, commonly known as New Deer, being wholly taken out of the parish of that name. From the notice in the statistical account, it would seem as if this was rather a rectification or modification of an old parish of Fetter-Angus, but no such parish is mentioned in the ancient lists, though there certainly was an old church there, which seems to have been a dependency of St. Fergus. The minister of the latter is said to have done duty occasionally at Fetterangus, as late as 1620. The first church was built in 1622, and about 30 years ago was replaced by the present structure.

STRICHEN, according to the Statistical Account, was erected into a

7

parish in 1627, "consisting of 38 ploughs, 32 of which were taken from Rathen, and 6 from Fraserburgh (the six ploughs of Saithly)." The old church was built in 1620, according to the author of the View of the Diocese of Aberdeen. That now in use dates from 1799.

PITSLIGO is the last erected parish. The lands of Pittendrum were formerly in the parish of Fraserburgh, and some farms belonged to that of Tyrie, which, in Boece's time, seems to have reached to the sea, but the greatest part belonged to Aberdour. from which it was disjoined on the application of Lord Pitsligo in 1630, when the church was built in 1632, but the carved belfry is said not to have been erected till 1635. The first minister was Andrew Cant, who, when transferred to Aberdeen by the General Assembly in 1640, makes rather a conspicuous figure in the pages of the local historian, Spalding, by his energy in forcing the puritan discipline on the re- cusant royalists. From him a writer in the "Spectator" would derive the word *cant*, as others do from the lingo of the Canterbury pilgrims, but a more obvious source is the chaunting of the old church service. Near the Castle of Pitsligo is a well dedicated to the Nine Maidens, who, Mr. Patrick Cook, in his account of the parish in 1723, thinks "may probably have been the Nine Muses." The Nine Maidens, how- ever, are decidedly of native extraction, and are well known in legend as the daughters of St. Donald or Donevald, a Scot, who, going into the country of the Picts, led a secluded life with his family in Glen Ogilvy, in Glammis, near Dundee. The church of Tough is dedicated to the Nine Maidens, that of Dalmaok, on Deeside, to Mazota or Mayok the eldest, and that of Echt to her younger sister, Fincana.

On their father's death, the nine virgins accompanied St. Bridget to Abernethy, and there formed a religious community in a house given them by the king. The legend is referred by different authors to the time of S. Palladius—of S. Columba, or of Nectan III., who introduced the Roman usages among the Picts, as we read in Bede. In his reign there is reason to believe that a religious house was established at Abernethy, but this might have been a restoration of some older foundation of a former prince of the same name, for we read in the Pictish Chronicles that in the third year of Nectan the son of Erip (an early king of the Picts), Darlugdach, a pupil of St. Bridget, and Abbess of Kildare, in Ireland, was an exile for Christ's sake in Britain, and in the second year of her sojourn, Nectan dedicated Abernethy to God and St. Bridget, in the presence of Darlugdach, who sang Allelulia over that offering.* Unless we refer the legend of the Nine Maidens to the earliest of the dates assigned, their leader, St. Bridget, cannot have been the famous Irish saint of that name, as she was a contemporary of St. Patrick; but by the legend of Mazota in the Breviary, the king had the church consecrated by St. Patrick, then staying in Scotland.†

I have only to observe in conclusion that the obscurity attaching to our parochial history is not due merely to the remote date and rude character of the age when it commenced, for we find it continues on to a comparatively recent period, and probably the different

---

* Skene's Chronicles of the Picts and Scots, p. 6.

† Pars Hyem. fol. xxiii.

changes of ecclesiastical regime from the reformation downwards, have had much to do with it, as well by leading to carelessness in the local records, as by the loss or dispersion of such as were actually made.

CPSIA information can be obtained
at www.ICGtesting.com
Printed in the USA
BVHW042015050519
547421BV00014B/982/P